Python Crash Course

By: PG WIZARD BOOKS

Step By Step Guide To Mastering Python Programming!

Python Crash Course: Step By Step Guide To Mastering Python Programming!

Table of Contents

Introduction

Learning a programming language can be a daunting task for many, but the right guidance can be the differentiator and the ultimate deciding factor as to how well you learn the language. Python is an easy to learn, high-level language which supports both structured and object-oriented programming.

This book aims at making the basic fundamentals of the language clear to the programmers. The dynamics of the language have been explained so as to enable developers to learn fine coding skills. Python has readable codes and an easy syntax thus making it simple to learn. It has automatic memory management system along with a comprehensive library that allows the programmers to write programs in a fewer lines of code as compared to other programming languages like C++ and Java.

Learning Python can be your stepping stone in the field of programming since Python methodologies can be used in a broad range of applications.

Lastly, the book is useful both for beginners who want to master this language and the experienced programmers who wish to revisit the basics or want a manual   for   reference.

We would like to thank you for downloading this book and we hope that the bookis valuablefor its readers.

Chapter 1: Preamble to Python

Python programming language was created by Guido Rossum in 1989. It is an object-oriented, multi-purpose and interactive scripting language. The language has been designed as highly readable. Python has fewer syntactical constructions and uses English keywords frequently. It is considered as a great language for beginners in the programming field.

Features of Python

1. Python provides rich data types and easier to read syntax as compared to other languages.
2. As compared to other programming languages it allows more run-time flexibility.
3. It is a platform independent scripted language with complete access to operating system API's.
4. Python libraries are cross-platform, thus making them compatible with Windows, MacIntosh and Linux.
5. It supports interactive mode that allows snippets of codes to be tested and debugged interactively.
6. It is a portable language and can run of various hardware platforms with same interface.
7. The Python source code can be easily maintained.
8. It provides support and an enhanced structure for big programs than shell scripting.
9. For building large applications, python can be assembled in to byte-code.
10. Python can be effortlessly incorporated with JAVA , C++, C , COBRA and Active X.
11. It can be used for programming video games, various scientific programs and artificial intelligence algorithms.
12. It has automatic memory management system.

Python is a self-sufficient language and consists of many tools and once the programmer becomes aware of their uses then it becomes an easy task for them. The language makes a solid foundation to branch out and learn other programming languages.

Python Crash Course: Step By Step Guide To Mastering Python
Programming!

Installing and Setting Up Python

Python distribution is available for wide range of platforms. It is easy to install and nowadays many Linux and Unix distributions include the latest version of Python. To download and install Python you can visit http://www.python.org/downloads/ and opt for the desired version. Even though version 3 is the latest but still Python 2 is used widely. Once you have downloaded and installed you need to set up the path. To add the Python directory for a particular session in-

Linux /UNIX –

   a) In the csh shell type setenv PATH "$PATH:/usr/local/bin/python" then press Enter.
   b) For Linux, in the bash shell, type export ATH= "$PATH:/usr/local/bin/Python" then press Enter.
   c) Type PATH="$PATH:/usr/local/bin/Python" in the sh or ksh shell and press Enter.
   d) Please note that /usr/local/bin/Python is the path of the Python directory.

Windows-

   a) Type path %path%;C:\Python at the command prompt and press Enter.
   b) The path of Python directory is C:\Python

Running Python

There are three different ways to start Python. Python can be started from DOS, UNIX or any other system that gives you a shell window or a command-line interpreter. You can right away start coding in the interactive interpreter-

        C: > python #Windows/ DOS
        Or
        python% #Unix/Linux
        or
        $python #Unix/Linux

A python script can be executed at command line by invoking the interpreter on your application.

IDE – Integrated Development Environment

You can run Python from GUI (Graphical User Interface) environment as well, provided you have a GUI application on your system that supports Python.

1. IDLE is the very first Unix IDE for Python.
2. For Python, PythonWin is the first Windows interface and is an IDE with a GUI.
3. From the main website the Macintosh version of python along with IDLE and IDE can be downloaded either as BinHex's files or MacBinary.

Make sure the Python environment is set up properly and is working fine so that you can execute your codes easily. (Python - Environment Setup)

Chapter 2: Basic Syntax

In the previous chapter, we learned how to install and set up Python. This chapter we will discuss the Python Syntax. A set of rules that defines how a program will be written and interpreted is called Syntax.

Let's understand various methods of programming

Interactive Mode Programming

At the command prompt type the below mentioned text and press Enter

print "Hello, Python!"

The output in version 2.4.3 will be *Hello,Python*!. Incase you are using the new version then you will have to use parenthesis along with the print statement–

print ("Goodmorning, Python!");

Script mode programming

The execution of script begins and continues till the script the finished upon invoking the interpreter with script parameter. As soon as the script finishes the interpreter will not be active any more. To understand it better take a look at this simple program.

Python files have extension **.py.** Type the source code *print "Hello, Python!"* in a test.pyf file and try to run the program as - *$ python test.py*. It will generate the following output –

Hello, Python!

Now presuming the availability of Python interpreter in /usr/bin directory, run
the program as-

$ chmod +x test.py   # to make the file executable

$ ./test.py

Output will be –

Hello, Python!

Identifies in Python

A name which is used to recognize a variable, class, function, module or other
subject in Python is called as an identifier. An identifier begins with a to z or A to
Z letters or a _ (underscore) which is followed more letters or a zero, digits (0 to
9) and underscores. No punctuation characters like %, $, @ are allowed within
Python identifiers. It is a case dependent language.

a) Class names begin with uppercase letters and all other identifiers begin
with a lowercase letter.
b) An identifier which begins with a single foremost underscore indicates that
it is private.
c) An identifier with two leading underscore denotes a strongly private
identifier.
d) The identifier is a language-defined special name in case it ends with two
trailing underscores.

Reserved Words

There are certain reserved words in Python which cannot be used as variable or a
constant or any other identifier name. All reserved words are in lowercase only.

not	exec	and
or	finally	assert
pass	for	break
print	from	class
raise	global	continue
return	if	def
try	import	del
while	in	elif
with	is	else
yield	lambda	except

Lines and Indentation

In Python, to indicate blocks of code for function and class definitions or flow control, there are no braces. The line indentation denotes the block of codes. In the indentation, the number of spaces is variable, but inside the block same amount of indentation should be done for all statements. Therefore, a block is formed by all the unbroken lines which have been indented with same number of spaces.

Multi-Line Statements

A new line in Python typically marks the end of a statement. However, the use of line continuation character (\) is allowed to denote the line should continue.
Example –
Total = goods_one + \
     goods_two + \
     goods_three + \
The line continuation character is not required for statements contained within brackets ( ), [ ] or { }.

Quotation

In python, all three quotes (' , " or """) are accepted. These indicate string literals provided the same kind of quote begins and closes the string. To cover the string across multiple lines, triple quotes are used.

Comments

The comment in Python begins with a hash (#) sign that is not within the string literal. After the hash all characters up to the end of the physical line form a part of the comment. However, they are ignored by the Python interpreter.

Blank lines

Blank lines are ignored by Python. These are the lines which have just whitespace, probably with a comment.

Multiple Statements on a Single line

On a single line multiple statements are allowed with a semicolon (;) provided that none of the statement starts a new code block.

Suites

In Python, a single code of block made by a cluster of statements is called as suites. The compound statements like if, else, while, def and class need a suite and a header line. The header lines start with statement (including keyword) and a colon denotes the end. They are trailed by one or more lines that make a suite.

Chapter 3: Python Fundamentals

Now that we know the syntax of Python, it is imperative for programmers to understand the python fundamentals. In other words, we would be discussing the basics on which the Python programming is based.

VARIABLES

A reserved memory location where values are stored is known as a variable. Memory space is allocated by the python interpreter and on the basis of data type of a variable it takes decision on what to store in this reserved memory. Hence, in the variables storing of characters, integers, or decimals is possible by assigning them different data types.

How to assign values to variables?

For assigning values to the variables you need to use the equal (=) sign. The left hand side operand denotes the variable name and the right side operand denotes the stored value inside the variable. Example –

counter = 10	(integer assignment)
miles = 100	(floating point)
name = "Tom"	(string)

print counter
print miles
print names

In the above example-10, 100 and Tom are the values assigned to counter, miles and name variables respectively and will give us the result as –
10
100
Tom

Assigning a lone value to numerous variables at the same time is also possible.

Example –
x= y= z= 1

In the above example, with value 1, the integer object is created, and same memory location is assigned to all three variables. Apart from this multiple objects can also be assigned to several variables. Like –
x, y, z = 1, 2, "Tom"

Data types

There are many types of data which are reserved in memory such as; age of a person is defined in numbers, and his address is defined as alphanumeric. To define the operations possible there are several standard data types which are used. We are just writing a brief on them as of now and these will be explained in detail in next chapters .They are –

a) Numbers – As the name suggests numeric values are stored in this data type. Upon assigning a value to them number objects are created. Various numerical types that supported by Python are–
   (1) Signed integers (int) e.g. – 2, 4, 44 etc.
   (2) Long integers (long), they can be depicted in hexadecimal and octal as well. e.g.- 0122L, -0x19323L etc.
   (3) Floating point real values (float) e.g. – 5.0, 2.22, -88.88 etc.
   (4) Complex numbers (complex) e.g. – 3e+26j, 45.j etc.

b) Strings –The adjoining set of characters depicted in quotation marks are called strings. Both single and double quotes are allowed in Python. The concatenation operator is represented as plus sign (+) and the repetition operator is represented as (*) asterisk.

c) Lists – These are mainly flexible data types in Python. The items in a list are separated by a comma and are written inside square brackets. The concatenation operator is represented as plus sign (+) and the repetition operator is represented as (*) asterisk.

d) Tuples - It is data type in sequence, similar to lists. A comma separates the number of values contained in tuples and unlike lists they are enclosed in parenthesis. Lists cannot be updated.

e) Dictionary – Dictionaries in Python are hash table types. They function like hashes or associative arrays and consist of key-value pairs. The dictionary keys are typically numbers or strings. The curly braces enclose

the dictionaries and by using ([ ]) square brackets values can be accessed
and assigned. For example, to create, add and delete entries in dictionary

 # make a phone book:
*phonebook = {'Tom Halter': 665544, *
*'Liza Raymond': 889966, 'Ronald Johnson': 776655, *
'Kim Lee': 443344}

 # add the person 'Mathew Peterson' to the phonebook:
phonebook ['Mathew Peterson'] = 99887766

del phonebook ['Kim Lee']

OPERATORS

The constructs which can manipulate the value of an operand are known as
operators.

Python operators

1. **Arithmetic**

   These operators execute various arithmetic calculations like addition,
   subtraction, division, multiplication, exponent, %modulus etc. For
   arithmetic calculation, there are various methods in Python like you can
   use the eval function, calculate and declare variable, or call functions.
   Let us take a simple example –
   a = 4
   b = 5
   print a + b

   Output will be "9". Similarly other arithmetic operators like division (/),
   multiplication (*), exponent (**) etc. can be used.

2. **Comparison**

   The comparison operator compares the value on either side of the operand
   to determine the relation between them. Various comparison operators are
   (!=, ==, >, <, <=, >=).

Example – we will compare the value of a to the value of b and print the result in true or false. Assume value of a =4 which is smaller than b =5. Now when we print the value as a >b, it actually compares the value of a to b and since it is incorrect, it returns as false. Similarly you can use other comparison operators.

3. Assignment

To assign the value of the right operand to the left operand, we use assignment operators.They are (+, +=, -=, /=, *=, %=, **=, //=). Example-

num1 = 4
num2 =5
print ("Line1 – Value of num1:" , num1)
print ("Line2 – Value of num2:", num2)

Output –

('Line1 –Value of num1:',4)
('Line2 – value of num2:', 5

4. Logical

These operators are used for conditional statements which are true or false.
AND, OR and NOT are the logical operators in Python
AND – it returns TRUE if both left and right operands are true.
OR – it returns FALSE if either of the operand is true.
NOT – it returns TRUE if operand is false

Example-
x = true
y = false
print ('x and y is', x and y)
print ('x or y is', x or y)
print ('not x is', not x)

The result will be –
('x and y is', False)

('x or y is', True)
('not x is', False)

5. Membership

Inside a sequence such as strings, lists or tuples membership is checked by these operators. These are of two types (in and not in). These operators give result based on the variable present in specified string or sequence.
Example –
We will check whether value of x=3 and y=7 is available in list or not by using membership operators.

x= 3
y =7
list = [1, 2, 3, 4, 5];

if (x in list):
    print "Line 1 – x is available in the given list"
else:
    print "Line 1 – x is not available in the given list"

if (y not in list):
    print "Line 2 – y is not available in the given list"
else:
    print "Line 2- y is available in the given list"

Result of the above code –

Line 1 – x is available in the given list
Line 2 – y is not available in the given list

6. Identity

Memory locations of two objects are compared by identity operators. They are of two types – is and is not.
is – it returns true if two variables point the same object otherwise false.
is not- it returns false if two variables point the same object, otherwise true.

Example –

x = 10

y = 10

if (x is y):

>   *print "x & y SAME identity"*

y = 20

if (x is not y):

>   *print "x & y have DIFFERENT identity"*

Following result is generated –
x&y SAME identity
x & y DIFFERENT identity

7. Bitwise

A bitwise operator work on bits and performs bit by bit operation. Python supports the following Bitwise operators - & Binary AND, | Binary OR, ^ Binary XOR, ~Binary Ones Complement, << Binary Left shift and >> Binary Right shift.

Operators Precedence

It determines which operator needs to be evaluated first. Precedence of operators is necessary to avoid ambiguity in values. For example – multiplication has a higher precedence than addition. Following operators are usedin Python – (**, ~+ -, */ % //, + -, & , ^|, >><<, &, <=<>>=, <> == !=, is is not, in not in , not or and)

STATEMENTS

Anticipating the conditions that might occur while executing a program and specifying the actions according to those conditions is called decision making. The decision structures assess numerous expressions which produce TRUE or FALSE as a result. You need to determine which action to take and what statements to execute if the result is TRUE or FALSE otherwise. In Python programming any non-zero and non-null values are assumed as TRUE, and if it is either null or zero then it is assumed as FALSE value.

Following types of decision making statements are provided in Python –

1. **if statements** - it contains a Boolean expression followed by one or more statements.
   A logical expression is used to compare the data and decision is made on the basis of comparison result. If Boolean expression evaluates to TRUE, then the block of statement(s) inside the *if* statement is executed. In case it evaluates FALSE, then the first set of code after the end of *if* statement is executed.

   Syntax –
   if expression:
     statement(s)

2. **if....else statements** – In this an *if* statement is followed by an optional *else* statement.If the conditional expression in the *if* statement resolves to FALSE value or 0, the block of code executes in an else statement.

   Syntax –
   if expression:
     statement(s)
   else:
     statement(s)

3. **elif statement** – It permits you to examine multiple expressions for TRUE and carry out a block of code as soon as one of the condition evaluates to TRUE. They are also optional statements and random number of *elif* statements following an *if* can be there.

   Syntax –
   if expression 1:
     statement(s)
   if expression 2:
     statement(s)
   elif expression3:
     statement(s)
   else:

statement(s)

4. **nested statements** – When you want to examine a different condition
   when a condition works out to be true then you can use *nested if*
   statements. Inside a nested if statement, an *if...elif ... else* inside another
   if...elif..else construct is also possible.

Syntax –
if expression1:
   statement(s)
   if expression2:
   Statement(s)
   elif expression3:
   statement(s)
   else:
   statement(s)
elif expression4:
   statement(s)
else:
   statement(s)

Chapter 4: Learn about Python loops, Strings, Lists, Tuples, and Dictionary

We have already introduced these terms in the previous chapter. Now we will take a look at each one of them in detail so that you can understand their usage in Python programming.

LOOPS

Typically the statements are executed in sequence, but if a situation arises when you are required to execute a block of code many number of times. In Python, a loop statement permits you to execute a statement or a group of statements numerous times. To handle the looping requirement following types of loops are available in Python –

1. **while loop** – this loop repetitively executes a target statement as long as the condition given is true.
   Syntax-
   while expression:
   *   statement(s)*

   Here, it can be a single statement or a block of statements and the condition may be an expression. The loop iterates as long while the condition is true. When the condition becomes false, the program control passes to the line immediately following the loop.

2. **for loop** – these loops have the capability to iterate over items of whichever sequence, like a string or list.
   Syntax-
   for iterating_var in sequence:
       statement(s)

   The sequence which contains an expression is evaluated first and then the first item in a sequence is assigned to the *iterating_var*. After this the statement block is executed. All the items in the list are assigned to *iterating_var*, and the statement(s) block is executed until the entire sequence is exhausted.

3. **Infinite loop–** If a condition never becomes FALSE it becomes an infinite loop. The results in a loop that never ends are called as infinite loops. These loops might be useful in client/server programming where server needs to run continuously for the client programs to communicate with it as and when required.

Using else statements with loops

If an else statement is used with for loop, then the else statement is executed when the loop has exhausted iterating the list. When else is used with a while loop, the else statement is executed when the condition becomes false.

Loop Control Statements

The execution from normal sequence is changed with loop control statements. So when execution leaves a scope, all automatic objects that were created in that scope are destroyed. Listed below are the control statements that are supported by Python –

a) **Break statement** – it ends the current loop statement and transfers execution to the statement immediately following the loop. The break statement can be used in both *for* and *while* loops. Most common use of break statement is when some external condition is triggered requiring a quick exit from loop.
Syntax-
break

b) **Continue statement** – The control is returned to the beginning of the while loop. The continue statements reject all the remaining statements in the current iteration of the loop and moves the control back to the top of the loop. It can be used for both *for* and *while* loops.
Syntax-
continue

c) **Pass statement** – When a statement is required syntactically but you do not want any command or code to execute, we use pass statement. It is a *null* operation and nothing happens on execution.
Syntax –
pass

STRINGS

In python, strings can be created by simply enclosing characters in quotes. The single quotes are treated same as double quotes. It is as easy as assigning value to a variable. Python has a built-in string called as 'str' which has many features. A literal in string can expand into multiple lines but there has to be back slash at the end of each line before the new line is created.

Example –
var 1 = 'Goodmorning World!'
var 2 = ' Python Programming'

How to access values in strings?

A character type is not supported by Python, they are considered as strings of length one, therefore also considered as substring. In order to access substring, the square brackets are used for slicing along with the index or indices.

Example –
var 1 = 'Goodmorning World!'
var 2 = "Python Programming"
print "var1[0]:", var1[0]
print "var2[1:5]:", var2[1:5]

result –
var1[0]: G
var2[1:5]: ytho

Updating Strings

Existing strings can be updated by (re)assigning a variable to another string. The new value can be related to a completely different string altogether or to its previous value.

String operators

There are various string operators, assume variable **a** holds 'Hello' and **b** holds 'World'

Operator	Description	Example
*	Repetition –it prints the character twice.	a*2 will give HelloHello
+	Concatenation- adds value on both sides and gives results	a + b will give Hello World
[:]	Range slice – gives characters from given range.	a[1:4] will give ell
[ ]	Slice – gives characters from given index	a[1]will give e
not in	Membership – if a character does not exist in a given string it returns true	M not in a will give 1
in	Membership – if character exists in the given string it returns true	H in a will give 1
r/R	Raw string- it surpasses actual meaning of escape characters	Print r'\n' prints \n and print R'\n' prints \n
%	Format – does string formatting	Read below

String formatting

The string formatting % operator is exclusive to strings and makes up for the bunch of having functions from C's printf family.

Example –
print "My name is %s and weight is %d kg!" % ('Alex', 25)

Result –
My name is Alex and weight is 25kg!

Triple Quotes

A triple quote in Python allows the strings to span in multiple lines which include verbatim TABs, NEWLINEs, and many other special characters. The syntax for triple quotes include three consecutive double or single   quotes.

Changing lower and upper case

In Python, you can change the string to upper case from lower case

str = "this is an example";
print "str.capitalize( ):", str.upper( )

Result –
str.capitalize( ): THIS IS AN EXAMPLE

LISTS

In Python, the fundamental data structure is a sequence. All the elements in a sequence are assigned a number; its index or position. In python, there are six built-in types of sequences and most common are tuples and lists.
Lists are the most flexible data type which can be written as a list of values separated by comma between the square brackets. The items in the list may not be of same type.

Example –
list 1 = ['english', 'french', 1996, 2015];
list2 = [1, 2, 3, 4, 5];
list3 = ["x", "y", "z"]

Just like string indices, list indices also start at 0, and list can be concatenated, sliced and so on.

How to access values in lists?

The square brackets are used for slicing along with the indices or index to get a value at the index.

list 1 = ['english', 'french', 1996, 2015];
list2 = [1, 2, 3, 4, 5, 6, 7];
print "list1[0]:", list1[0]

print "list2[1:5]:", list2[1:5]
Result –

list1[0]: English
list2[1:5]: [2, 3, 4, 5]

Updating Lists

Multiple elements or a single element of lists can be updated by giving the slice on the left-hand side of the assignment operator. It is possible to add elements in a list by using the append( ) method.

Example –

list = ['english', 'french', 1996, 2015];
print "Value available at index 2:"
print list[2]
list[2] = 2016;
print "New value available at index 2:"
print list[2]

Result –

Value available at index 2:
1996
New value available at index 2:
2016

Deleting elements from list

By using either the remove( ) method if you don't know which element to delete or del statement if you know exactly which element(s) you are deleting you can delete a list element.

Example –

list = ['english', 'french', 1996, 2015];

print list1
del list1[2];

print "After deleting value at index 2:"
print list 1

Result-

['english', 'french', 1996, 2015]

After deleting value at index 2:
['english', 'french', 2015]
Similar to Strings, lists also react to * and + operators; they mean repetition and concatenation here as well, except that the outcome is a new list, not a string. As the lists are sequences, slicing and indexing also works in a similar manner as in strings.

Python has some built-in list functions –
1. cmp(list1, list2) – it compares elements in each list
2. max(list) - it returns item from the list with maximum value.
3. len(list) – it gives total strength of the list.
4. min(list)- it returns items from the list with minimum value.
5. List(seq) – it converts tuple into list.

List methods –
1. list.append(obj)- it appends object obj to list
2. list.extend(seq) – it appends the contents of seq to list
3. list.count(obj) – it returns count of how many times obj occurs in list.
4. list.insert(index,obj) – it inserts obj into list at offset index.
5. list.index(obj)- it returns the lowest index in the list that obj appears.
6. list.remove(obj) – it removes object from list
7. list.pop(obj=list[-1])- it removes and returns the last obj from list.
8. list.sort([func]) – sorts objects of list, use compare function if given
9. list.reverse( )- it reverses object of list in place.

TUPLES

The series of unchangeable Python objects are called as tuples. They are sequences similar to lists. Unlike lists, you cannot change tuples and they make use of parentheses, on the other hand square brackets are used in lists. You can create tuples by simply separating values with a comma and optionally these values which are separated by comma can be put inside parentheses.

Example –

tup1 = ('english', 'french', 1996, 2015);
tup2 = (1, 2, 3, 4, 5);
tup3= "x", "y", "z";

Two parentheses consisting of nothing; *tup= ( );* denotes an empty tuple.

In order to write tuple that contains single value a comma needs to be included, even though there is barely a single value; *tup1= (45,);*

How to access values in Tuples?

Make use of the square brackets for slicing, besides the index or indices to get the value available at the index.

Example –
tup1 = ('english', 'french', 1996, 2015);
tup2 = (1, 2, 3, 4, 5, 6, 7);

print "tup1[0]:", tup1[0]
print "tup2[1:5]:", tup2[1:5]

result –

tup1[0]: English
tup2[1:5]: [2, 3, 4, 5]

How to update tuples?

Since tuples are unchangeable you cannot change or update the tuple elements values. You can take parts of existing tuple to make new tuples.

Example –

Tup1 = (14, 32.44);
Tup2 = ('xyz', 'abc');

#Below action is not valid for tuples
#tup1[0] =100;

Therefore let's create a new tuple

tup3 = tup1 + tup2;
print tup3

result –

(14, 32.44, 'xyz', 'abc')

Deleting elements in tuples

Individual elements of tuples cannot be removed. However, there is nothing
wrong in positioning together one more tuple with the undesired elements
discarded. In order to completely remove a tuple, just add **del** statement.

Example –

tup = ('english', 'french', 1996, 2015);

print tup
del tup;
print "After deleting tup:"
print tup

Result –

('english', 'french', 1996, 2015)

After deleting tup:
Traceback (most recent call last):
 file "test.py", line 9, in <module>
  print tup;
NameError: name 'tup' is not defined

Please note that an exception is raised because after del tup tuple does not exist.

Similar to strings, tuples react to * and + operators; they denote repetition and concatenation here too, but a new tuple is created as a result and not a string. The indexing and slicing in tuples works in a similar way as it works in strings.

Following are the built-in functions of tuples –

1. cmp(tuple1, tuple2) – it compares the elements in each tuple
2. max(tuple) – it returns item from the tuple with maximum value.
3. len(tuple) – it gives the total length of the tuple.
4. tuple(seq)- it converts a list into a tuple.
5. min(tuple) – it returns item from the tuple with minimum value.

PYTHON DICTIONARY

Dictionary values can be of any kind, but the keys must be of an unchangeable data type such as numbers, strings and tuples.

How to access values in Dictionary?

By using the square brackets along with the key to obtain its value dictionary elements can be accessed.

Example –

dict = {'Name': 'Tom', 'Age': 10, 'Class': 'Fifth'}
print "dict['Name']:", dict['Name']
print "dict['Age']:", dict['Age']

Result –

dict['Name']: Tom
dict['Age']: 10

Properties of Dictionary Keys

a) Per key you cannot have more than one entry, i.e. duplicate key is not allowed. The preceding assignment wins when a duplicate key is encountered.

b) Keys should be unchangeable. By this it means that you may utilize numbers, strings or tuples as dictionary keys but something like ['key'] is not allowed.

Built-in dictionary functions-

1. cmp(dict1,dict2) – compares elements in both
2. str(dict)- produces a printable string
3. len(dict) – gives total length of dictionary
4. type(variable) – returns the type of passed variable.

Built-in dictionary methods-

1. dict.clear( ) – removes all elements of dictionary
2. dict.fromkeys( )- creates a new dictionary with keys from seq and values set to value
3. dic.copy( ) – returns a shallow copy of dictionary
4. dict.get(key, default=None) – returns value or default if key not in dictionary.
5. dict.has_key(key) – returns true if key in dictionary*dict*, otherwise false
6. dict.keys( )- returns list of dictionary dict's keys
7. dict.items( ) – returns a list of *dict's* tuple pairs
8. dict.setfedault(key,default=None) – similar to get, but will set dict[key]= default if *key* is not already in dict.
9. dict.values( )- returns list of dictionary *dict's* values.
10. dict.update( )- adds dictionary *dict2's* key-values pair to *dict*

Chapter 5: Insight into Python Functions, Modules and Classes

FUNCTIONS

A block of code that is organized, reusable, and is used to carry out a single, related action is called as a function. The functions provide better modularity for your application and a high degree of code reusing. Python has many built-in functions but creating your own functions is also possible and these are called as *user-defined* functions.

How to define a Function?

In order to give the necessary functionality you can define a function. Here, are some simple rules for defining a function in Python –

1. A function block begins with the keyword def followed by the function name and parentheses (( )).
2. Any arguments or input parameters must be positioned within these parentheses. Parameters can also be defined within these parentheses.
3. Inside every function the block of code starts with a colon and is indented.
4. The statement return [expression] exits a function, optionally passing back an expression to the caller. The return statement with no arguments is the same as return None.
5. The first statement of a function can be an optional statement; the documentation string of the function or *docstring*.

Syntax –
def functionname (parameters):
  "function_doctsring"
  function_suite
  return [expression]

Parameters, by default have a positional behavior and you need to inform them in the similar order as they were defined.

How to call a function?

31

By defining a function you only give a name to a function, structures the block of
code and specify the parameters that are to be included in the function. Once the
basic structure of a function is finalized, you can execute it by calling it from the
Python prompt directly or from another function.

Example of function printme( ) is as below –

```
# Function definition is here
def printme(str):
    "This prints a passed string into this function"
    print str
    return;
```

```
# Call the printme function now
printme ("This is first call to user defined function!")
printme ("This is second call to the same function")
```

Output –
This is first call to user defined function!
This is second call to the same function

In Python, all parameters (arguments) are passed by reference. This means what
a parameter refers to inside a function, if you change it, the change gets reflected
back in the calling function.

Function Arguments

By using following types of arguments you can call a function –
  a) Required arguments –these are the arguments passed to a function in
     correct positional order. In this the number of arguments in the function
     call should exactly match with the function definition.
  b) Keyword arguments – These are related to function calls. Once keyword
     argument is used in a function call, the parameter name identifies the
     arguments to the caller. This allows for skipping of arguments or places
     them out of order since the keywords given to match the values with
     parameters is used by the Python interpreter.
  c) Default arguments –in the function call if a value is not provided for the
     argument this argument assumes a default value.
  d) Variable-length arguments – While defining a function it may be required
     to process a function for additional arguments than specified, these are

called as variable-length arguments. Unlike default and required arguments, they are not named in the function definition. The variable name that carries the value of all non-keyword variable arguments an asterisk is placed before it. Tuple will remain empty in case there are no extra arguments specified during a function call.

Scope of Variables

In a program, all variables may not be accessible at all locations. This depends on where you have declared a variable. The portion of the program where you can access a particular identifier is determined by the scope of variables. There are two basic scopes –
   a) Global – Variables that are defined outside the function body have a global scope. These can be accessed throughout the program body by all functions.
   b) Local – Variables that are defined inside the function body have a local scope. These can be accessed only inside a function in which they are declared.

MODULES

Modules help in organizing the code logically. The code becomes easy to use and understand by grouping the related code into module. A Python object with arbitrarily named attributes that can bind and reference is called module. In simple words, module is a file that consists of Python code. It can define variables, functions, and classes.

Example of simple module support.py -

```
def print_func( par ):
    print " Hi:", par
    return
```

Import Statememt

Any Python source file can be used as a module by executing an import statement in some other Python source file.

Syntax –

import module1[, module2[,. . .moduleN]

<u>From import statement</u>

Specific attributes can be imported from a module into the current namespace
with the help of *from import* statements.

Syntax –
from modname import name1[, name2[,. . .nameN]]

<u>From...import * statement</u>

The *from..import*statement* makes the import of all names possible from a
module into the current namespace.

from modname import*

Locating Modules
The module is searched by the Python interpreter in the below mentioned
sequence when a module is imported.
   a) Current directory
   b) In case the module isn't found, the Python looks into every directory in the
      shell variable PYTHONPATH
   c) The default path is checked in Python, if else fails.

The module search path is stored in the system module sys as the
sys.pathvariable. This variable contains the current directory, PYTHONPATH,
and the installation dependent default.
PYTHONPATH – it is an environment variable, which consists of a list of
directories.
Syntax-
For windows -
set PYTHONPATH=c:\python20\lib;

For UNIX-
set PYTHONPATH=/usr/local/lib/python

Namespaces and scoping

A namespace is a dictionary of variable names (keys) and their corresponding objects (values)

Variable can be accessed in Python in both local and global namespace. In case a global and local variable has the same name, the global variable is overshadowed by the local variable. All functions have their own local namespace. The same scoping rules are followed by classes as ordinary functions. Whether variables are global or local is a informed guess made by Python. An assumption is made that any variable is local which has been assigned a value in a function. Therefore, for assigning a value to a global variable inside a function, the global statement needs to be used first. The statement *global VarName* tells that VarName is global. Searching the local namespace for the variable is stopped by Python.

The dir( ) function-

It returns a systematic list of strings consisting of the names defined by a module. List consists of all the functions, modules and variables that are defined in a module.

The globals( ) and locals( ) functions-

These functions can be used to return names in the local and local namespaces depending on the location from where they are called. If from inside a function a globals( ) is called, it will return all the names that can be globally accessed from that function. In case locals( ) is called from inside a function, it will return names that can be locally accessed from that function. The return type for both the functions is dictionary. So the names can be extracted using the keys( ) function.

The reload( ) function

The code in the top level portion of a module is executed only once when the module is imported into a script. However, if you want to execute the top level code again, then use the reload( ) function. A previously imported module is imported again by this function.

Syntax –

reload(module_name)

35

In syntax, *module_name* is the name of the module to be reloaded and not the string consisting of the module name.

CLASSES

As we know that Python is an object-oriented language, therefore using and creating objects and classes is easy. A class is a user-defined model for an object that defines a set of attributes that portray any object of the class. The attributes are the data members and methods, associated via dot notation. Data member is an instance variable or a class variable that holds data related with a class and its objects. The instance variable is a variable that is defined inside a method and belongs to the current instance of a class.

How to create classes?

A new class definition is created by a *class* statement. The name of the class straight away follows the keyword *class* followed by a colon.

class ClassName:
  'Optional class documentation string'
  class_suite
- A class has a documentation string, which can be accessed via ClassName._doc_.
- Each component statement that defines class members, functions and data attributes exist in the *class_suite*.

How to create instances of class?

Use class name to call the class and pass in no matter what arguments its _init_ method accepts for creating an instance of a class.

How to access attributes?

Dot operator with object need to be used in order to access the object's attributes.

Built-in class attributes

Dot operator can be used to access the built-in attributes–

a) _dict_ - dictionary containing class's namespace
b) _name_ - class name
c) _doc_ - class documentation string or none, if undefined.
d) _bases_ - probably a vacant tuple containing the base classes in the order of their occurrence in the base class list.
e) _module_ - the module name in which class is defined. This attribute in interactive mode is "_main_".

Garbage Collection

In Python, to make the memory space free, objects (class instances or built-in) that are not required are deleted automatically. Garbage collection is a method by which Python from time to time recovers memory blocks that are no longer in use. Python's garbage collector runs while the program is being executed and is triggered when an object's reference count reaches zero. An object's reference count increases when it is positioned in a container (tuple, list or dictionary) or is assigned a new name. The object's reference count decreases when it is deleted with *del,* its reference goes out of scope or it is reassigned. Python automatically collects when an object's reference count reaches zero.

Class inheritance

A pre-existing class can be used for deriving and creating a new class instead of begining from scratch by listing the parent class after the new class name inside parentheses. The attributes of its parent class are inherited by the child class, and these attributes can be used as if they were defined in the child class. Just like their parent class the derived classes can be declared. Though, after the class name a list of base classes to inherit from is given.

Syntax –

class SubClassName (ParentClass1[, ParentClass2,. . .]):
    'Optional class documentation string'
    class_suite (Python - Environment Setup)

Chapter 6: Exception handling

<u>Exception</u>

An event that interrupts the standard flow of the program's instructions at the time of execution is called as an exception. Typically, when such a situation is encountered by a Python script that it cannot handle, it raises an exception. In other words, an exception is a Python object that depicts an error. When an exception is raised in Python script, it either the exception is handled immediately or it is terminated.

<u>How to handle an exception?</u>

In case you find a suspicious code in a program, then the program can be defended by putting that code in a **try:** block. After this include an **except:**statement followed by a block of code which manages the problem as gracefully as possible.

Syntax –

try:
  You do your operations here;
  ....
except Exception I:
  If there is Exception I, then execute this block.
Except Exception II:
  If there is Exception II, then execute this block.

  ....
else:
  If there is no exception then execute this block.

Please note –
- A single try statement can have multiple except statements.
- A generic except clause can also be provided, which manages any exception.
- An else-clause can also be included after except clause(s). If the code in try: block does not raise an exception the code in the else-block is executed.

- A better place for code that does not need the try: block's protection is the else-block.

Except Clause with no exception —all the exceptions that occur are caught by the try-except statement. However, it doesn't make the programmer recognize the root cause of the problem that may occur.

Except clause with multiple exceptions- the same except statement to handle multiple exceptions can be used.

Try-finally clause – The finally: block with try: block can be used. In the finally block you can place any code that must execute, irrespective of the fact that the try-block has raised an exception or not.

Argument of an exception – An argument is a value that gives more information about the problem and an exception can have an argument. You can catch an exception's argument by providing a variable in the except clause.

Raising Exceptions

You can raise exceptions in several ways by using the raise statement.

Syntax –

raise [Exception [, args [, traceback]]]

Here, *argument* is a value for the exception argument and *Exception* is the type of exception. However, argument is optional; if not supplied, the exception argument is None. For example, an exception can be a class, string or an object. Most exceptions that Python core raises are classes, with an argument that is an instance of the class.

In Python, you are allowed to create your own exceptions by deriving classes from the standard built-in exceptions. (Python Exceptions Handeling)

Conclusion

This brings us to the end of this edition of the book. We can easily say that Python is a powerful language and that is the reason why all big companies are looking for programmers who have the knowledge of this dynamic language.

Before we end, let's summarize on what we have learned so far. The book began with basic introduction to Python, its features, how to install and set up. We also understood that Python has fewer syntactical constructs thus making it easy and readable. All Python fundamentals i.e. variables, data types, operators, lists, strings, loops, tuples and dictionary have been covered in the book.

We have also ensured that the concept of function, classes, and modules is covered for a better understanding of the language. The last section on exception handling can be useful in practical application.

To conclude, we can say that once you are clear on the basics of Python you will be able to create almost anything you want.

Thank you once again for downloading this book, hope it has given you a meaningful insightinto Python.

Works Cited

Python - Environment Setup. n.d. 2017.
<https://www.tutorialspoint.com/python/python_environment.htm>.

Python Exceptions Handeling. n.d. 2017.
<https://www.tutorialspoint.com/python/python_exceptions.htm>.

www.ingramcontent.com/pod-product-compliance
Lightning Source LLC
LaVergne TN
LVHW052125070326
832902LV00038B/3952

Python Crash Course: Step By Step Guide to Mastering Python Programming

Want to learn Python Programming? Need to learn it?

Want to be able to do programming quick and easy?

Learn the step by step of Python loops, strings, lists and tuples?

PG Wizards gives you modules to work through!

You will get all your basic information as well for all new programmers!

Such as Syntax and beyond!

Whether your just starting out or looking to reinforce your current skills? Perfect either way everything & anything you could think ab

The most economical buys that will get you all you need to know to learn Python programming quickly and efficiently!

PG WIZARDS BOOKS

ISBN 9781544955964
90000 >
9 781544 955964